Losing your baby teeth is a real sign that you are growing up. Very soon, new, grown-up teeth will take the place of the teeth you have lost. While you are waiting, the Tooth Fairy may pay you a visit.

This book tells you all about the Tooth Fairy. She will give you good advice, too, on looking after your teeth. Then there is a place for you to keep a record of your lost teeth – and your new teeth.

Best of all, there is a special little bag for you to pop your lost tooth into and put under your pillow. While you are asleep, the Tooth Fairy will do her magic and change it into a special little treat – just for you.

My Tooth Fairy Book

Written by
Nicola Baxter

Illustrated by
Cathie Shuttleworth

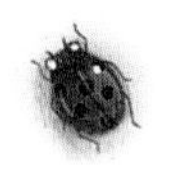

Published in 1997 by
Armadillo Books
An imprint of Bookmart Limited
Desford Road, Enderby,
Leicester LE9 5AD, England

Reprinted 1998, 1999 (twice), 2000

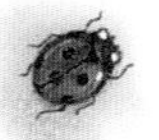

ISBN 1-90046-519-1

Produced for Bookmart Limited by Nicola Baxter
Printed in Malaysia

Contents

The Tooth Fairy's Story

Fairies are very generous little people. They love to give presents and treats to grown-ups and children. Sometimes we get so used to these presents that we hardly notice them. The Leaf Fairy makes sure that autumn leaves are really dry and curly, so that when you walk through them, they make a lovely rustling sound. The Dawn Fairy teaches the birds to sing their early morning songs, so that children everywhere can wake up to the sound of music.

So each fairy has a job to do and there are so many nice things in the world for children to enjoy that fairies have a very busy time.

But once there was a fairy who had nothing to do at all! She wanted so much to make children happy but everything she thought of was already being looked after by an older and wiser fairy. All day long she flew through the fields and lanes, looking for a task that needed her special attention. Then, one day, she heard a very sad sound.

It was a little boy, sitting on his bed and crying. The fairy perched on the window sill to find out what was the matter.

"Oh, dear!" sobbed the little boy, "my tooth has come out and left a hole in my mouth! I don't like it!"

The fairy was very upset. The poor little boy! How could she help him?

Just then, the little boy's mother came into the room. She gave the little boy a hug and explained that he would soon have a big, new, grown-up tooth to take the place of his lost baby tooth.

"You've only lost one tooth because something better will come in its place," she explained.

This gave the listening fairy a very good idea. Perhaps if the little boy had a present now, while he was waiting for his new tooth to grow, he would feel better! And if one little boy was upset about losing his tooth, perhaps there were lots of other children who needed a surprise treat too!

The fairy realised that she needed someone older and wiser to help her to decide what to do next. She flew off as fast as her wings would carry her in search of the kindest person she knew, the Rainbow Fairy.

Now the Rainbow Fairy lived high up in the sky and the little fairy was very tired when she arrived. But she was so excited about her idea that she didn't even think of resting. Instead, she started at once to tell the Rainbow Fairy about the little boy and his lost baby tooth.

"Not so fast!" laughed the Rainbow Fairy. "Now, sit down on this little cloud and tell me all about it."

“I’d like to help all the children who are sad when their baby teeth fall out,” explained the little fairy, “even though they will soon grow new, grown-up teeth.”

“That sounds like a lovely idea,” said the Rainbow Fairy. “But how are you going to know when teeth are lost? They are tiny things and you cannot search everywhere each day to find them.”

The little fairy looked sad. “You’re right,” she said. “Whatever am I going to do?”

The Rainbow Fairy smiled kindly. “Well,” she replied, “you had a very good idea about helping the children in the first place. I am sure that if you think about this a little bit, you will soon solve the problem. Do come back and see me if I can help some more.”

So the little fairy flew back down to earth and sat down under a tree to think. The world seemed a very big place for one little fairy to search.

Then, just as she was beginning to think that her idea would never work at all, something fell ... BUMP! ... on the ground beside the little fairy. It was an acorn! The shiny acorn sat snugly in its own little cup. The little fairy looked at it and slowly a big smile came over her face. “That’s it!” she cried.

"Children need somewhere special to put their lost teeth," said the fairy to herself. "Then I will know where to look for them and where to leave a present for the children. A special little cup, like an acorn cup, would be a good idea. I must go and see the elves at once!"

Now elves are very clever little people. They make all the things that fairies need, and they are very good at using bits and pieces that are not needed any more. Have you ever wondered what happens to all the tiny things you lose?

Well, you will probably find that somewhere a little elf has made something really useful from your lost pencils and pins and beads.

When the little fairy arrived at the elves' workshops, everyone was very busy, but the youngest elf came forward to see how he could help.

"Could you make me some little cups for children to put their lost teeth in?" asked the fairy. "They would need to be big enough to hold any kind of tooth."

"Hmm," sighed the elf, "that might not be easy."

"You see," he explained. "Everyone else is very busy, but I'm still doing my training. I haven't learnt to make little cups yet. So far, I've only learnt how to sew and make things from cloth and thread."

The little fairy thought for a moment. "Well," she said, "could you make me some little bags that a tooth would fit into? I would want them to be very nicely made, of course."

"That would be no problem at all!" laughed the youngest elf. "And just look here! I have some lovely velvet material left over from the curtains in the Fairy Queen's palace. Would that be suitable? I could make lots and lots of little bags from this."

The little fairy stroked the cloth. "That would be perfect," she said. "How long will all the work take you?"

"I'll start at once!" cried the youngest elf.

And before the little fairy could say another word, he got out his scissors.

All day long, the little elf snipped and sewed, while the little fairy helped him as much as she could.

Before long, it began to get dark. The little fairy lit all the lanterns she could find and the youngest elf worked on.

By the time that the moon had risen in the sky, there was a pile of little bags ready for the fairy.

"You can close them with these gold threads," explained the elf. "Just pull them tight and tie the tassels in a bow. Then the tooth inside can't fall out and get lost."

The little fairy was overjoyed. "These are perfect!" she cried.

In the morning, the elf wrapped the bags in a net of fine cobwebs, and the little fairy flew off with them to show the Rainbow Fairy.

"She will be so pleased that I had another good idea!" laughed the little fairy, as she flew higher and higher.

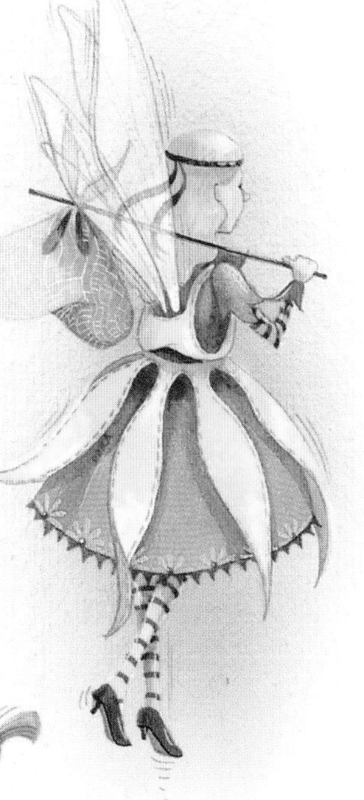

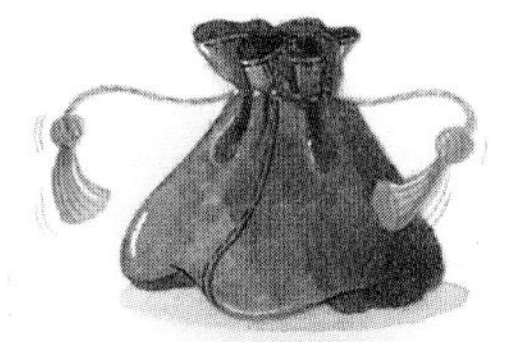

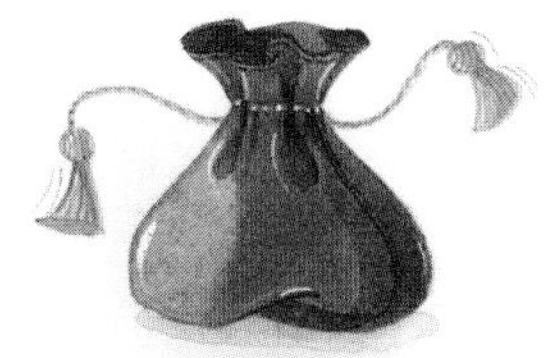

When she saw the little bags that the youngest elf had made, the Rainbow Fairy laughed out loud.

"You certainly have been thinking hard," she said, "and working hard too! Well done, little fairy. Now you deserve a new name. We will call you the Tooth Fairy! But there is just one more thing that you will need to do."

"What is that?" asked the Tooth Fairy.

"You will need to explain to children about the little bags and make sure that all those who want one have one," explained the Rainbow Fairy. Seeing the Tooth Fairy's face, she laughed again. "Don't worry," she said, "this is where my special magic will be very useful."

The Rainbow Fairy waved her arms and fluttered her wings. The sky around her was filled with rainbow colours.

"Now," said the Rainbow Fairy kindly, "fly down to the end of the rainbow and you will find something to help you. Hurry now, there are lots of children waiting for you!"

So the little Tooth Fairy flew down right to the end of the rainbow, and at the bottom she found a silver box, shining in the coloured light. Very carefully, she undid the lid and looked inside.

Can you guess what she found there?

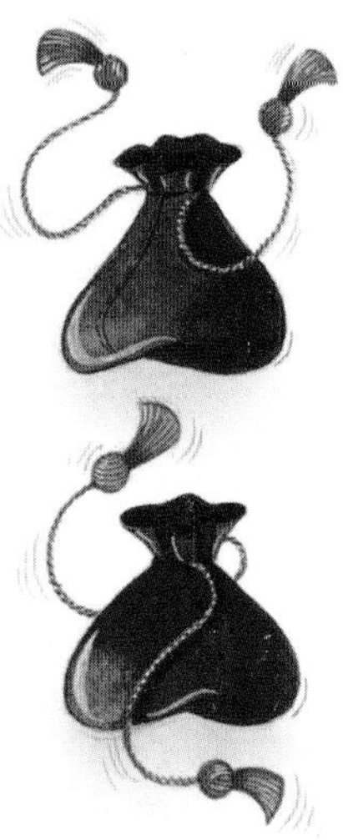

It was this book! A special book, telling children all about the Tooth Fairy and giving them their very own little bag to put each lost tooth inside.

Just ask a grown-up to cut along the top of the little pocket in the front of the book. Then put your tooth in the velvet bag and hide it under your pillow when you go to sleep.

The little Tooth Fairy is very busy these days, but she's sure to find time to visit you and leave a little treat. Sleep well!

The Tooth Fairy's Advice

Your new teeth are the ones that you will have for the rest of your life, so it is very important to look after them as well as you can. On the next pages, you will find some good ideas about how you can take care of your teeth.

Taking care of your baby teeth is important too. Your new teeth are growing underneath them, waiting to push your baby teeth out of the way when they are ready.

1 Go to see your dentist every six months. Dentists know even more about teeth than Tooth Fairies do! The dentist will look inside your mouth and make sure that your teeth are growing properly. It won't hurt at all, but you will know that a real expert has checked that everything is fine.

2 Brush your teeth at least twice a day. You will need your own special toothbrush. Your dentist or another grown-up will show you how to brush up and down, so that your teeth and gums stay healthy and strong. Remember to brush the ones at the back as well!

3 Try not to eat too many sweet, sticky things. The sugar sticks to your teeth, and they can begin to be damaged. Brushing your teeth will help to make sure that the sugar is cleaned away, but eating fewer sweet things will help too.

    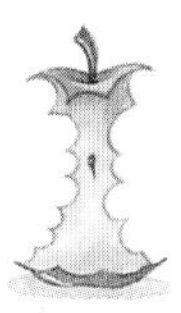

4 Remember what your teeth are for! They are for chewing up your food, not biting through string or chewing the tops of pens. Sports-players and motorbike-riders wear special helmets to protect their teeth – they know that they are not for catching cricket balls or munching mud with either! If you are careful with your teeth, they will last as long as you need them.

My name

Draw a picture or paste a photograph of yourself here.

My New Teeth

Everyone is different. And everyone's teeth are different too! You may lose your teeth before your friends do or not until months afterwards.

It is fun to keep a note of when you lose your baby teeth and when your new teeth grow through. It is amazing how quickly you will forget about it as you grow up. Fill in the spaces on the next two pages, and you will have a record to look at in the future, when the Tooth Fairy visits your own children!

I grew my first tooth when I was ______ years and ______ months old.

(You will need to ask someone who knew you as a baby about this!)

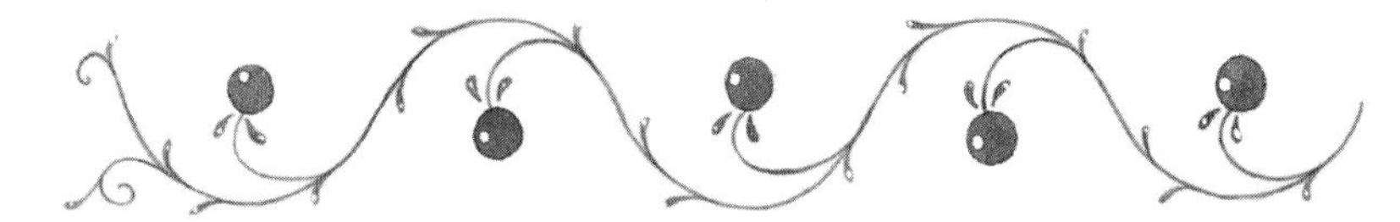

I lost my first baby tooth on _________day, the _____ of ________________ , __________.

The Tooth Fairy brought me ______________________
____

My first grown-up tooth began to show on

__________day, the _____ of _______________________ ,

__________, when I was ______ years and ______

months old.

The Tooth Fairy also visited me on the following

dates, when I lost more of my baby teeth.

__________________________ __________________________

__________________________ __________________________

__________________________ __________________________

Remember the Tooth Fairy

When you lose a tooth, you may be so excited that you forget about the Tooth Fairy! Don't worry, it is not too late to see if she will visit you.

As soon as you remember, pop the tooth in the little bag from the front of this book and put it under your pillow when you go to sleep. It's a good idea to tell the other people in your family that you have done this, so that they are not surprised if they hear the flapping of the Tooth Fairy's wings in the night.

The Tooth Fairy is rather shy. She is very happy to help children everywhere, but she doesn't like to be seen herself. So make sure that you shut your eyes tight and go to sleep as soon as you can. If she sees that you are awake, or just pretending, the Tooth Fairy may decide not to visit you this time.

Sometimes the Tooth Fairy is very busy indeed. As she says herself, she is only a little fairy and she cannot fly very fast. If it seems that she has forgotten you, leave the bag under your pillow for a few days. She will certainly try to come soon.

What should you do if you lose a tooth but cannot find it? Don't worry! Ask a grown-up to help you write a little note for the Tooth Fairy, explaining what has happened. Pop that into the bag instead – she's sure to understand.

Most important of all, don't forget that the Tooth Fairy will be able to tell if you have been taking care of your teeth properly and following the advice she has given you. When she is very busy, she visits children who clean their teeth carefully first of all. Make sure you are one of those, won't you?